See It Grow

PUMPKIN

WITHDRAWN

by Jackie Lee

Consultant: Karen C. Hall, PhD
Applied Ecologist, Botanical Research Institute of Texas
Fort Worth, Texas

BEARPORT
PUBLISHING

New York, New York

Credits

Title Page, © topseller/Shutterstock; TOC, © Le Do/Shutterstock and © Ian 2010/Shutterstock; 4–5, Mustafanader/Dreamstime; 6T, © schankz/Shutterstock; 6–7, © Alena Brozova/Shutterstock; 8, © YuriyBoyko/Shutterstock; 9, © Marina Onokhina/Shutterstock; 10–11, © OperationShooting/Shutterstock; 12–13, © orangecrush/Shutterstock; 14, © Aleksandr Volkov/Alamy; 15, © Maria Dryfhout/Shutterstock; 16, © syaochka/Shutterstock; 17, © imagesbycat/Shutterstock; 18, © Terry Wilson/iStock; 19T, © ryasick/iStock; 19M, © Brittny/Shutterstock; 19B, © princessdlaf/iStock; 20, © olgaman/Shutterstock; 21, © MarilynVolan/Shutterstock; 22T, © Linda Kloosterhof/iStock; 22B, © Suzannah Skelton/Thinkstock; 23 (T to B), © Madlen/Shutterstock, © Stockagogo/Shutterstock, © Craig Barhorst/Shutterstock, © AlenaBrozova/Shutterstock, and © Yuriy Boyko/Shutterstock; 24, © topseller/Shutterstock.

Publisher: Kenn Goin
Editor: Natalie Lunis
Creative Director: Spencer Brinker
Design: Debrah Kaiser
Photo Researcher: Olympia Shannon

Library of Congress Cataloging-in-Publication Data

Lee, Jackie, active 2015, author.
  Pumpkin / by Jackie Lee.
      pages cm. — (See it grow)
  Includes bibliographical references and index.
  ISBN 978-1-62724-840-2 (library binding) — ISBN 1-62724-840-4 (library binding)
  1. Pumpkin—Juvenile literature. I. Title. II. Series: See it grow.
  SB347.L44 2016
  635'.62—dc23
                                        2015008704

For more information, write to Bearport Publishing Company, Inc., 45 West 21st Street, Suite 3B, New York, New York 10010. Printed in the United States of America.

10 9 8 7 6 5 4 3 2 1

Contents

Pumpkin

In the fall, pumpkins are everywhere!

They are round and orange.

How did they get that way?

Pumpkins can be different sizes. Some are as small as tennis balls. Others are as big as washing machines.

Every pumpkin starts out as a seed.

When the seed is in the soil, it starts to grow.

First, **roots** reach downward.

seed

roots

Then a **shoot** pokes up out of the ground.

shoot

A plant's roots take in water and **nutrients** from the soil.

Soon, two little leaves appear.
They are called **seed leaves**.

seed
leaves

Next, two new leaves start to form.

They are called **true leaves.**

Leaves use sunlight to help make food for the plant.

true leaves

9

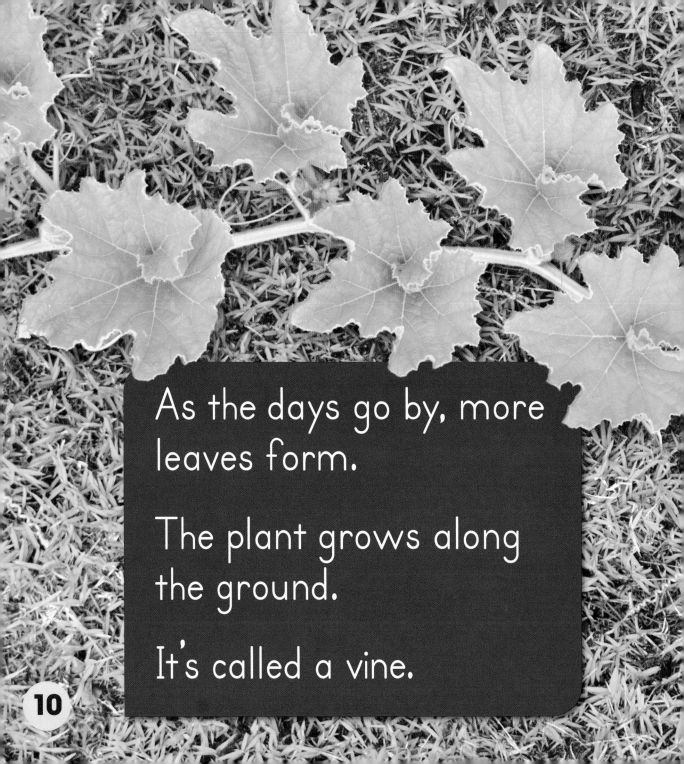

As the days go by, more leaves form.

The plant grows along the ground.

It's called a vine.

A pumpkin vine can grow 30 feet (9 m) long.

Yellow flowers appear on the vine.

Some flowers have something round at the bottom.

It's a baby pumpkin!

baby
pumpkin

Once the pumpkin
starts growing bigger,
the flower dies.

The baby pumpkin gets bigger and bigger.

Soon it's the size of a baseball.

After a while, it starts to turn orange.

stem

A thick stem attaches the pumpkin to the vine.

The pumpkin keeps getting bigger.

It becomes orange all over.

Now it's **ripe**.

16

Many pumpkins can grow on one vine.

What do people do with
ripe pumpkins?

They cut them open
and remove
the seeds.

18

Some pumpkins are carved into jack-o'-lanterns for Halloween.

The seeds can be roasted and eaten.

Pumpkins are also used to make pies.

19

What else can you do with
the seeds?

Save a few to plant next spring.

They will grow into new
pumpkin plants!

Some people grow pumpkins on huge farms.

Pumpkin Facts

- Pumpkins are a type of squash.

- Pumpkins grow in places with warm summers and cool fall weather.

- The world's biggest pumpkins weigh more than 1,000 pounds (454 kg).

- Not all ripe pumpkins are orange. Pumpkins can also be white, pale green, or even blue.

Glossary

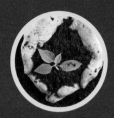 **nutrients** (NOO-tree-uhnts) substances that plants get from the soil, which they need to grow and be healthy

 **ripe** (RIPE) fully grown and ready to be picked

 **roots** (ROOTS) plant parts that take in water and food from the soil

 **seed leaves** (SEED LEEVZ) leaves that were tucked inside a seed

 **shoot** (SHOOT) a young plant that has just appeared above the soil

 **true leaves** (TROO LEEVZ) leaves that start growing on a young plant

Index

Read More

Esbaum, Jill. *Seed, Sprout, Pumpkin Pie (Picture the Seasons).* Washington, DC: National Geographic (2009).

Pfeffer, Wendy. *From Seed to Pumpkin (Let's-Read-and-Find-Out Science).* New York: HarperCollins (2012).

Learn More Online

To learn more about pumpkins, visit
www.bearportpublishing.com/SeeItGrow

About the Author

Jackie Lee lives in upstate New York, where many pumpkins grow each year.